DOLPHINS

by Sylvia M. James

Photo Credits:
Cover, p. 12: © DiMaggio/Kalish/Corbis Stock Market; back cover: © Tim Davis/Corbis Stock Market; pp. 1, 4 (top right), 5 (top right), 7 (Bottlenose), 15 (center), 18, 20, 22: © Gerard Lacz/Animals Animals; p. 4 (left): © Johnny Johnson/Animals Animals; pp. 4 (bottom right), 7 (Rough-toothed): © James Watt/Animals Animals; p. 5 (left): © Rob Lewine/Corbis Stock Market; p. 5 (bottom right): © Lester Lefkowitz/Corbis Stock Market; pp. 6 (Hawaiian Spinner, Atlantic Spotted, Common), 10, 19, 24: © Michael S. Nolan/Wildlife Images/Tom Stack & Associates; p. 6 (Southern Right Whale): © Ingrid Visser/Seapics.com; p. 6 (Indo-Pacific Humpbacked): © Thomas Jefferson/Seapics.com; p. 6 (Irrawaddy): © Roland Seitre/Seapics.com; p. 7 (Heaviside's): © Todd Pusser/Seapics.com; p. 7 (Fraser's, Clymene): © Robert L. Pitman/Seapics.com; p. 7 (Hector's): © Brandon Cole/Norbert Wu Productions; pp. 7 (Striped), 14: © Doug Perrine/Seapics.com; p. 8 (top left, bottom): © Roland Seitre/Peter Arnold, Inc.; p. 8 (top right): © Gregory Ochocki/Photo Researchers, Inc.; p. 9: © Donna McLaughlin/Corbis Stock Market; p. 11: © Henry Ausloos/Animals Animals; pp. 13, 17: © Brian Parker/Tom Stack & Associates; p. 15 (lower left): © Rob van Nostrand; p. 16: © Mark Stouffer/Animals Animals; p. 20: © Laurel Ehrlich/Dolphin Research Center, Inc., Grassy Key, Florida; p. 21: © James Watt/Norbert Wu Productions; p. 23: © Norbert Wu/Norbert Wu Productions.

Illustrations on pages 13 and 23 copyright © 2002 by Pedro Julio Gonzalez under exclusive license to MONDO publishing. All rights reserved.

Text copyright © 2002 by Sylvia M. James

MONDO Publishing
980 Avenue of the Americas
New York, NY 10018
Visit our website at www.mondopub.com

Printed in China

10 11 12   11 10 9 8

ISBN 1-59034-010-8
Designed by Annette Cyr

Library of Congress Cataloging-in-Publication Data

James, Sylvia M.
   Dolphins / by Sylvia M. James
      p. cm.
   Summary: Provides introductory information to the dolphin including its body parts and life cycle.
   ISBN 1-59034-010-8 (pbk.)
      1. Dolphins--Juvenile literature. [1. Dolphins.] I. Title

QL737.C432 J36 2002
599.53--dc21

                                        2001054402

CONTENTS

What Is a Dolphin?

Humpback Whale

Orca (whale)

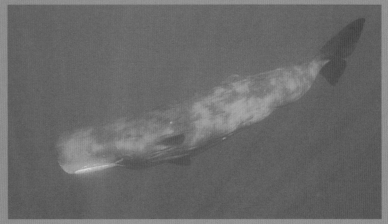

Sperm Whale

Dolphins are small whales.
All whales are mammals.

Humans, dogs, and cows are all mammals, too.

St. Bernard (dog)

Human

Holstein (cow)

There are 26 kinds of dolphins that live in the oceans.
Here are some of them.

Atlantic Spotted Dolphin

Hawaiian Spinner Dolphin

Indo-Pacific Hump-backed Dolphin

Common Dolphin

Southern Right Whale Dolphin

Irrawaddy Dolphin

Bottlenose Dolphin

Fraser's Dolphin

Hector's Dolphin

Rough-toothed Dolphin

Striped Dolphin

Heaviside's Dolphin

Clymene Dolphin

There are some dolphins that live in rivers.

Ganges River Dolphin

Amazon River Dolphin (Boto)

Yangtze River Dolphin (Baiji)

Dolphins eat fish and squid.

Parts of a Dolphin's Body

dorsal fin ⎯⎯⎯⎯

⎯⎯⎯ tail flukes

flippers ⎯⎯⎯⎯

A dolphin has fins, flippers, and a strong tail.

A dolphin moves its tail up and down to swim.

A dolphin's skin is smooth and slippery.

A dolphin has blubber under its skin to keep warm.

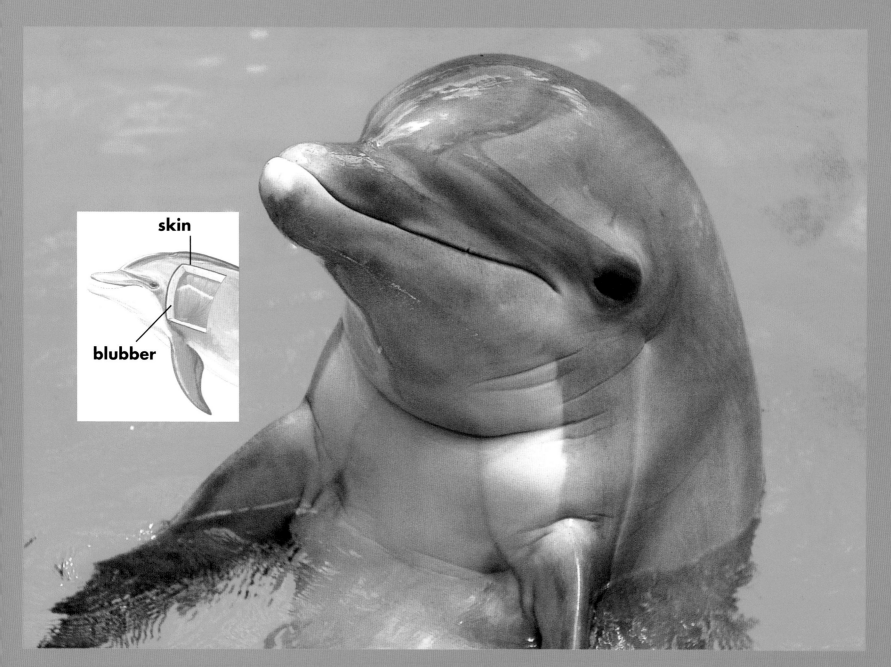

skin

blubber

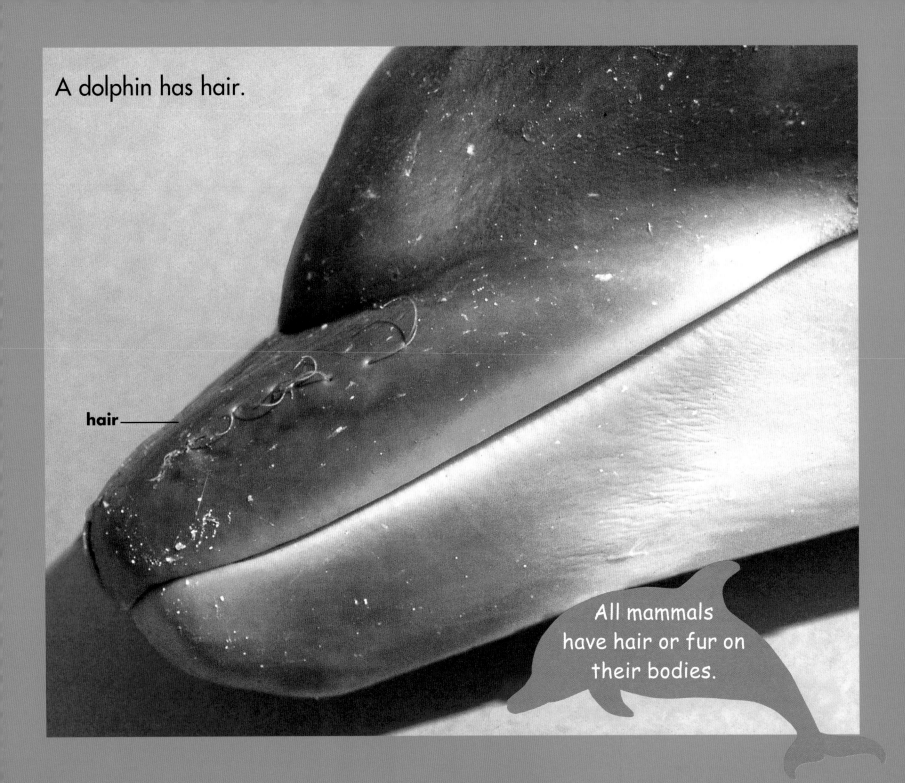

A dolphin has hair.

hair————

All mammals have hair or fur on their bodies.

14

A dolphin's mouth is called a beak. The beak is full of sharp teeth.

beak

teeth

A dolphin can have up to 130 teeth.

A human can have up to 32 teeth.

A dolphin breathes through the blowhole on the top of its head.

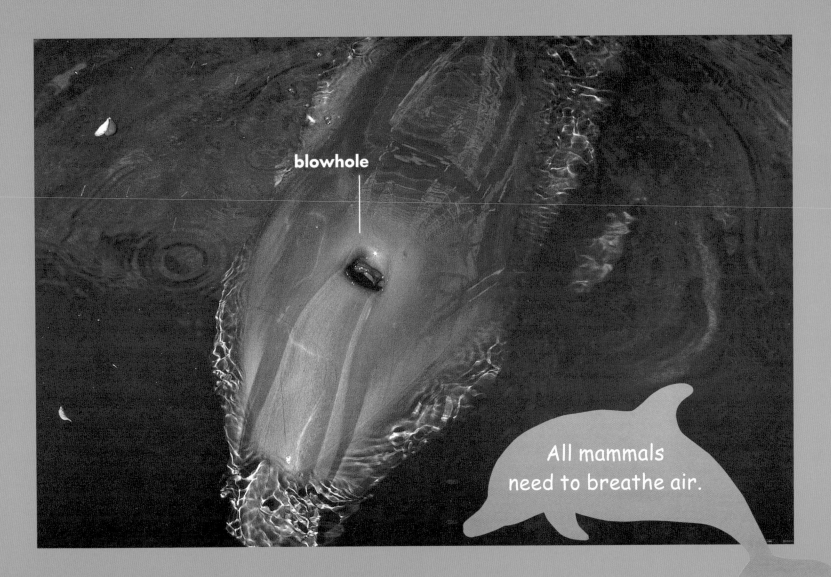

blowhole

All mammals
need to breathe air.

When a dolphin goes under the water, the blowhole shuts.

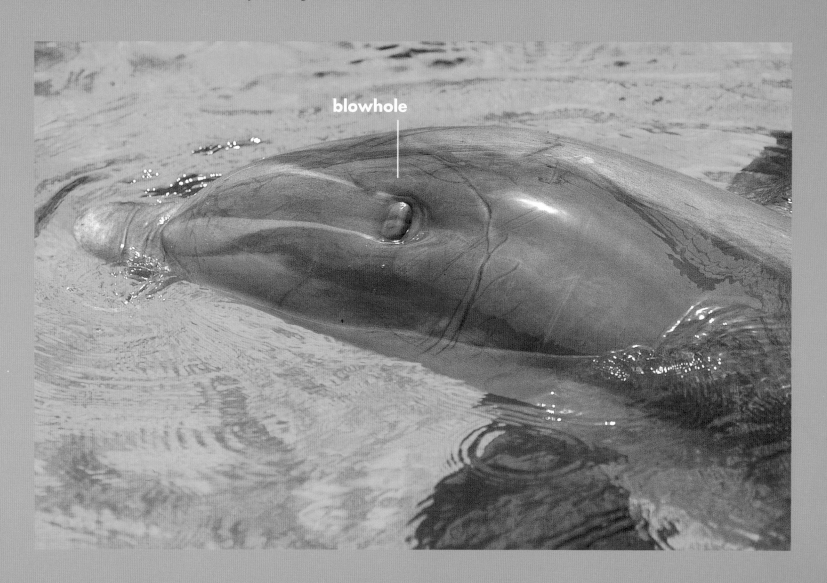

blowhole

Baby Dolphins

A baby dolphin is called a calf.

A mother dolphin only has one calf at a time.

A calf is born underwater. The mother pushes the calf up to the surface so it can breathe.

A calf drinks milk from its mother.

All mammals
can drink milk
from their mothers.

Dolphin Sounds

blowhole ———

A dolphin makes many sounds. The sounds come from its blowhole.

The sounds a dolphin makes help it find food to eat.

sound waves

Dolphins also use sound to find other dolphins.

A group of dolphins is called a pod.